Contents

Some words are shown in bold, **like this**. They are explained in the glossary on page 23.

What is a square?

A square is **flat** shape.

It is a special kind of **rectangle**.

Finding Shapes

Squares

Diyan Leake

www.raintreepublishers.co.uk
Visit our website to find out more information about **Raintree** books.

To order:
 Phone 44 (0) 1865 888112
Send a fax to 44 (0) 1865 314091
 Visit the Raintree Bookshop at **www.raintreepublishers.co.uk** to browse our catalogue and order online.

First published in Great Britain by Raintree, Halley Court, Jordan Hill, Oxford OX2 8EJ, part of Harcourt Education.
Raintree is a registered trademark of Harcourt Education Ltd.

© Harcourt Education Ltd 2006
First published in paperback in 2007
The moral right of the proprietor has been asserted.

Editorial: Diyan Leake
Design: Joanna Hinton-Malivoire
Picture research: Maria Joannou
Production: Victoria Fitzgerald
Originated by Dot Gradations Ltd
Printed and bound in China by South China Printing Company

10 digit ISBN 1 844 21333 1 (HB)
13 digit ISBN 978 1844 21333 7 (HB)
10 09 08 07 06
10 9 8 7 6 5 4 3 2 1

10 digit ISBN 1 844 21350 1 (PB)
13 digit ISBN 978 1844 21350 4 (PB)
10 09 08 07
10 9 8 7 6 5 4 3 2 1

British Library Cataloguing in Publication Data
Leake, Diyan
516.5
Finding Shapes: Squares
A full catalogue record for this book is available from the British Library.

Acknowledgements
The publisher would like to thank the following for permission to reproduce photographs: Corbis p. **12** (Craig Lovell); Getty Images pp. **5** (Imagebank/Kaz Mori), **13** (Imagebank/Cyril Isy-Schwart), 21 (Photodisc), **23** (straight, Imagebank/Kaz Mori); Harcourt Education Ltd pp. **6** (Malcom Harris), **7** (Tudor Photography), **8** (Tudor Photography), **9** (Malcolm Harris), **10** (Malcolm Harris), **11** (Malcolm Harris), **15** (Malcolm Harris), **16** (Tudor Photography), **17** (Malcolm Harris), **18** (Malcolm Harris), **19** (Malcolm Harris), **22** (Malcolm Harris), **23** (cube, Malcolm Harris; edges, Malcolm Harris; faces, Tudor Photography; solid, Malcolm Harris), back cover (cube, Malcolm Harris); Rex Features p. **14** (Dave Penman)

Cover photograph reproduced with the permission of Corbis

Every effort has been made to contact copyright holders of any material reproduced in this book. Any omissions will be rectified in subsequent printings if notice is given to the publishers.

The author and publisher would like to thank Patti Barber, specialist in Early Years Education, University of London Institute of Education, for her advice and assistance in the preparation of this book.

The paper used to print this book comes from sustainable resources.

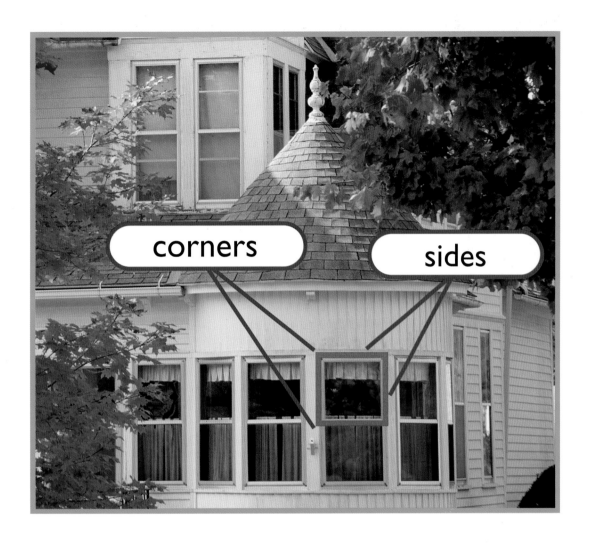

corners

sides

Squares have four corners and four **straight** sides.

All the sides are the same length.

Can I see squares at home?

There are lots of squares at home.

Some of them are in the living room.

Some birthday cards are square.

What other squares can you see
at home?

There are squares in the kitchen.

Some squares are big and some are small.

There are squares in the bathroom.

The square white tiles are smooth and shiny.

Can I see squares at school?

There are lots of squares at school.

You can climb the bars in the gym.

These boards have squares on them.

The squares are red, yellow, blue, and green.

Are there squares in the park?

This playground is in a park.

There are squares on the climbing frame.

Some of the plants in this park are planted in squares.

Different plants are different shades of green.

What do patterns with squares look like?

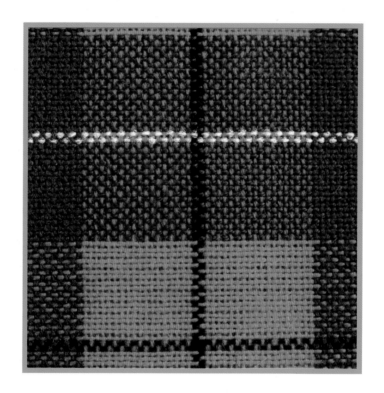

This cloth has a pattern of squares on it.

Cloth like this is used for blankets and rugs.

This board is for playing games.

It has a pattern of blue squares and yellow squares on it.

Can I see squares on other shapes?

faces

You can see squares on a **cube**.

A cube is a **solid** shape with square **faces**.

edges

Cubes have six square faces.

They have **straight edges**.

Are there cubes at school?

These bricks are **cubes**.

You can make a tall tower with them.

Dice are cubes.

They have spots on each **face**.

Can I play games with squares?

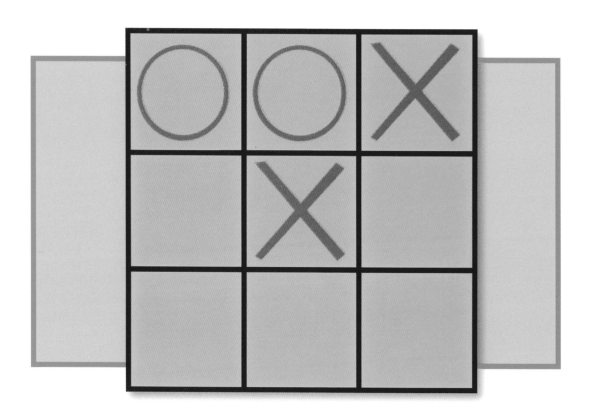

You can play noughts and crosses with a friend.

You try to get three in a row.

Each domino has two squares with dots on them.

You can set them up and topple them down.

Can I make squares out of other shapes?

See how many ways you can make squares!

Glossary

cube
shape with six faces that are all the same size

edges
lines where two faces of a shape come together

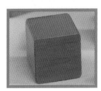
faces
the outside parts of a shape

flat
has no thickness to it

rectangle
flat shape with four straight sides and four corners

solid
has thickness to it, not flat

straight
not bent or curved

Index

Note to parents and teachers

Reading non-fiction texts for information is an important part of a child's literacy development. Readers can be encouraged to ask simple questions and then use the text to find the answers. Each chapter in this book begins with a question. Read the questions together. Look at the pictures. Talk about what the answer might be. Then read the text to find out if your predictions were correct. To develop readers' enquiry skills, encourage them to think of other questions they might ask about the topic. Discuss where you could find the answers. Assist children in using the contents page, picture glossary, and index to practise research skills and new vocabulary.